# AROUND
# SKIPTON-IN-CRAVEN
## IN OLD PHOTOGRAPHS

# AROUND
# SKIPTON-IN-CRAVEN
## IN OLD PHOTOGRAPHS

COLLECTED BY
## FRIENDS OF THE CRAVEN MUSEUM

ALAN SUTTON

Alan Sutton Publishing Limited
Phoenix Mill · Far Thrupp · Stroud · Gloucestershire

First published 1991

**British Library Cataloguing in Publication Data**

Around Skipton in old photographs.
I. Craven Museum
942.841

ISBN 0-86299-970-7

In memory of Dr Arthur Raistrick
co-founder of the Craven Museum

Typeset in 9/10 Korinna.
Typesetting and origination by
Alan Sutton Publishing Limited.
Printed in Great Britain by
The Bath Press, Avon.

# CONTENTS

# INTRODUCTION

Of pre-Domesday antiquity, Skipton – the Saxon *Scep-tun* or Sheeptown – lies in the fertile valley of the River Aire at the junction of routes passing north to south, and east to west.

It is described in William I's 1089 survey as 'Terra Regis', having been confiscated by him from Edwin, son of the Earl of Mercia, and is stated to be 'Waste Land'. This condition has been attributed by some historians to the ravages of the Danes, by others to the incursions of the Scots, and by further chroniclers to the 'Harrying of the North' by William himself.

Whoever the perpetrators, the condition of the whole of Yorkshire was at that time recorded as 'so fearful that the contemporary writers seem to lack words to set forth its full horrors.' (Freeman on the *Harrying of the North*.)

The 'Honour' of this waste land was granted by the king to Robert de Romille, one of his staunchest supporters, and whose association with the district is commemorated in the designation of the moorland to the east of the town as 'Rombalds Moor'.

The pragmatic de Romille, appreciating the strategic advantages of the town over more picturesque locations in his 'Manor', established his castle stronghold on the high ground at the head of what is now the main street. It is impregnable from the rear and with clear command of all approaches on the other three sides.

The original castle was rebuilt, extended and refurbished by his successors in title until its final restoration by Lady Anne Clifford after 'slighting' at the termination of the Civil War.

Also at the head of the spacious High Street is the parish church of the Holy Trinity. There is no record of a church before the Norman Conquest, the first mention being in 1120. This building too has been modified, extended and refurbished after suffering Civil War bombardment and the hazards of fire and lightning. It is known that there were bells before 1616, a record of that date referring to the need to replace the bell frame which was old. The clock was installed before 1803, necessitating the removal of the old gallery, and the porch was added in 1866. Inside the church there are innumerable memorials including the impressive Clifford tombs, and the stained glass eastern window by Capronier of Brussels.

A grammar school was endowed by Peter Toller in 1492, re-endowed by William Ermysted in 1548 and, still bearing his name, continues on a site to which it moved in 1877. Over the years elementary schools were established by some churches, these having been absorbed into the state education system. Denominational provision of school places was so satisfactory in Skipton that there was no need for a board school in the town.

A Mechanics' Institute was established in 1847, meeting originally in a room behind the Hole in the Wall inn, now a part of the Craven Court shopping precinct. (A part of this precinct also housed the Old Skipton Theatre where Edmund Keane and Harriet Mellon – Duchess of St Albans – are reputed to have played.) The institute moved to the old town hall or Toll Booth in Sheep Street and finally, with the assistance of the Carnegie Trust, built the public library, and science and art school (Craven College) now in the possession of the county council.

The town has evolved slowly, some might even say too slowly, from being purely agricultural, with some five hundred inhabitants, to an important market town. After the death of Lady Anne Clifford, administration of the area devolved into the hands of absentee landlords which gave rise to strong contemporary criticism that the needs of the locality were not being given full consideration. This may well have been true in the short term, but in the long term, the refusal of the Lords of the Manor to sell land or to enter into long-term leases for industrial development saved the town from the excesses of the Industrial Revolution.

The topographical situation in what is known as the Aire Gap had given ease of communication in all directions. The road system was augumented by the construction of the Leeds–Liverpool Canal, followed by the main lines of the London, Midland and Scottish Railway (formerly the 'Midland'), with express passenger and freight services from London to Edinburgh, Glasgow and Heysham Harbour – a link with Ireland and Irish cattle. These improvements in communications were accompanied by increased industrial potential, but this was always under the control of the Lords of the Manor.

The increasing need for cattle market facilities resulted in 1906 in the weekly 'Fair', traditionally held in the High Street, being moved on to land at the rear of the town hall (now a public car park). Soon a further purpose-built market was opened near the railway station in Broughton Road; this in turn was superseded in 1990 by a bigger modern auction mart off Gargrave Road, the Broughton Road site being developed by Morrisons as a supermarket.

The early predominance of sheep breeding and trading evolved through the cottage industries of spinning and weaving to a thriving textile industry. But with the arrival of the Leeds–Liverpool Canal cotton became the primary raw material processed and a closer association with East Lancashire was established. The workers in the new branch of the textile industry were herded into factories, some of which were eventually established in Skipton. The most famous of Skipton cotton products was Dewhurst 'Sylko' thread, used all over the world.

The post-war years have seen the decline of the textile industry throughout the country and Skipton has shown no exception to this trend. In 1945 there were some seven or eight factories, some operating as individual companies, others offering looms and power to smaller concerns. There are now only one or two textile manufacturers remaining. The close proximity of that geological phenomena the 'Craven Fault' provides viable facilities for extensive sandstone and limestone quarrying in the area and current road works support some continued activity in this sphere. Skipton, however, continues to prosper, situated at a junction for all forms of transport; it is recognized as the 'Capital of Craven' and the 'Gateway to the Dales', a centre for trade and tourism. The villages of Gargrave, Bradley, Cross Hills, Sutton, Carleton, Embsay, Draughton, Marton, Kildwick, Farnhill and Bolton Abbey are all part of Craven and enjoy a close association with the larger town. Each have their own individual traditions and characteristics, and would each warrant, and adequately reward, an hour or two of further investigation.

The following selection of photographs has been collected by the Friends of the Craven Museum, a body formed to support the local museum, housed in the town hall at Skipton and open to members of the public free of charge. The photographs depict buildings, places and people and will, it is hoped, revive memories for many, and give information to many others about the local environment and life style of the not too distant past.

Walter E. Walker
July 1991

# The Town

HIGH STREET on 'Cow Monday'. A cattle market was held in the town's main thoroughfare every week until 1906. This photograph was probably taken shortly before that date. William Mattock, hay and straw dealer, whose Middle Row premises are shown on the left, was also the proprietor of the High Corn Mill. An 1898 guidebook makes a point of mentioning that the two sets of premises were 'connected . . . by telephone'.

THE HEAD OF SKIPTON HIGH STREET, showing the parish church of the Holy Trinity and also the War Memorial erected in 1921.

RAIKES ROAD, looking towards the parish church. The building on the right was Wrights mineral water factory.

SKIPTON CASTLE from the tower of the parish church. The de Romille family began the building of the castle probably very early in the twelfth century. Prominent in the picture is the thirteenth-century gatehouse.

THE EASTERN PART OF SKIPTON CASTLE, built in 1536 by the First Earl of Cumberland for the reception of his son's bride, Lady Eleanor Brandon, the niece of King Henry VII.

SKIPTON CASTLE from the north. The excellent defensive possibilities of the site are obvious. The castle was twice besieged, during the Pilgrimage of Grace and in the Civil War between King Charles I and Parliament, when it was defended by Royalists from 1642 to 1645. When the garrison surrendered on 21 December 1645, the troops were allowed to march out with full military honours in recognition of their heroic conduct.

THE SPRINGS CANAL and Mill Bridge. The Springs Canal was constructed in 1773 to transport limestone from Lord Thanet's quarry at the back of Skipton Castle to the Leeds–Liverpool Canal. The building to the left of the bridge is the New Ship Inn. William Holdsworth is the earliest recorded landlord of this inn, in 1799. He died 'inebriate' in the same year.

MILL BRIDGE over the Springs Canal. Note the widening of the bridge which is obvious from below. In the overhang on the right, Skiptonians used to queue for fish and chips sold at the adjacent shop.

THE FISH AND CHIP SHOP at Mill Bridge and, on the right, the corn mill which gave the bridge its name.

THE CASTLE INN near Mill Bridge with a flock of sheep on its way back to the Dales from the turnip fields of the East Riding. In the foreground are farmers with brooms, waiting to sweep up after the sheep had moved on. Note the drinking cup on the wall of the parish church on the right.

BACK WATER STREET, now Back-o-the-Beck, with the Springs Canal in the foreground, the overflow of which runs into the Eller Beck.

BACK-O-THE-BECK, from the west end.

LOOKING DOWN UPPER COMMERCIAL STREET towards Christ Church (in the distance) and the former Primitive Methodist chapel. This building has had several uses since ceasing to be a place of worship in 1879; one of the last was serving as the fire station. Upper Commercial Street was demolished in 1964.

THE CANAL BASIN at the Springs Canal junction. The sheds on the right have been replaced by a chandlery. The Leeds–Liverpool Canal, which had a great impact on the industry and life of Skipton, reached the town in 1773. Construction had begun in 1770, but it was not open along its entire length until October 1816.

THE END OF BROOK STREET, formerly a quiet corner of Skipton.

COTTAGES ON OTLEY ROAD, since demolished.

STREET, SKIPTON.   1886

HIGH STREET in 1935. The first car was driven through Skipton in 1907; twenty-eight years later motor vehicles were making a great impact on the scene.

THOMPSON'S YARD, the last area of the High Street with dwelling houses. It was demolished in the 1960s to make way for the clinic, now local government premises. The yard took its name from Thomas Thompson, hatter and sexton, who lived at 7 High Street and built a few cottages on land at the rear, leased to him from the castle.

Sheep Street, Skipton.                    Published by A. B. Carter, Skipton.

SHEEP STREET. The steps on the right lead up to the door of the old town hall, a sixteenth-century building, superseded in 1862 by the present town hall. The old town hall became successively the Mechanics' Institute and the Friendly Societies hall, while the basement served as the town gaol for many years. It is now business premises. Note the interest in the photographer.

THE TOP OF THE HIGH STREET before 1910. The trees were planted to mark the Diamond Jubilee in 1897. On the left is the only four-storeyed building in the High Street.

THE PUBLIC LIBRARY was built on this site and opened on 16 February 1910.

A HORSE FAIR in the High Street in the 1930s. On the right can be seen the Carla Beck Milk Bar, opened in the early 1930s by the Hudsons of Carla Beck Farm, Carleton and believed to be the first milk bar in England.

COW AND CALF FOR SALE in the High Street. Stone setts were replacing cobbles at the time when this photograph was taken.

ALBERT STREET looking towards the High Street which can be reached through the archway in the centre. On the right are the premises of George Leatt, a notable international dog judge.

ALBERT STREET, formerly Spencer's Yard, during the demolition, in 1956, of Devonshire House which stood behind a high wall on the left. The shop on the right was Mrs Spence's confectioners. Note the setts and flagstones. Albert Street has since been demolished.

KENDAL'S YARD off the High Street, before 1957. The building at the bottom of the yard was once a theatre where Edmund Kean and Harriet Mellon, later Duchess of St Albans, are said to have acted. The yard, one of the earliest in Skipton, was named after John Kendal, landlord of the Hole in the Wall for many years.

KENDAL'S YARD, looking towards the High Street. The yards grew up when cottages were built on what were once long gardens at the rear of the High Street premises.

SKIPTON WORKHOUSE, later Raikeswood hospital, built in 1839/40 at a cost of six thousand pounds to serve forty-seven townships of the Skipton Union. In 1852 a local man named Benson Bailey wrote of the 'cleanliness, comfort and cheerfulness' which prevailed among the inmates. Skipton workhouse had a good reputation.

GARGRAVE ROAD, going out of the town to the north-west. The side entrance to the former Woodmans Inn is on the right near the gas lamp. Note the high-wheeled pram and the fourth girl on the left of the group who holds a 'bowl' (hoop).

SWEEPS YARD. On the left are the slaughterhouses of Mr Schultz, pork butcher on Middle Row. John Ackernley, the first sanitary inspector appointed by the local council, is in the distance, under the high wall on the right.

BIRTWHISTLE'S YARD, built at the rear of the Birtwhistle property in Caroline Square. The Birtwhistles were a well-known family of drovers and cattle-dealers, the most famous of whom was John Birtwhistle, thought to have been the first drover to travel to the Hebrides and the north of Scotland to bring cattle to the English market. He flourished between about 1740 and 1770. This yard was demolished in 1955.

QUEEN'S COURT, later known as Laycock's Yard. Thomas Spencer, co-founder of Marks & Spencer, was born in this yard in 1851. In the 1957 Report on the Sanitary Condition of Skipton it is described as being partly flagged and partly paved and very clean. There were four privies to eight houses, which was not a bad provision in a mid-nineteenth-century town.

KEIGHLEY ROAD before 1924. On the left is the narrow bridge over the Eller Beck which has now been culverted, the old Unicorn Hotel, some shops and then a row of five houses with gardens. The tall building beyond the houses is the Liberal club. The first building on the right is Meakin's shoe shop, then follows a gent's urinal in stone, and beyond it Miss Laurence's drapery.

DEVONSHIRE PLACE, looking from Keighley Road. On the left is the Eller Beck with a ford for vehicles (in the centre of the picture) and stepping-stones for pedestrians. The barn on the left was the workshop of Mr Friend, painter and decorator, and leading fireman. On the right is Drummond's, the plasterers.

BROUGHTON ROAD MILL, built in 1897 by the Skipton Room and Power Co. Ltd. The mill was badly damaged by fire in 1958. 'Owd Bill's' Garage, founded by William Wiseman, is in the foreground.

KEIGHLEY ROAD with the entrance to the Premier cinema on the left.

KEIGHLEY ROAD with the Premier cinema on the left. Built in 1913, it was the first purpose-built cinema in Skipton and was known locally as 'Scratters'. By the time this photograph was taken it had become the Dales Discount House. It was demolished in 1979.

SACKVILLE STREET with a small shop at the end of every street coming into it from the left. The third shop from the left was Plews, the well-known pork butchers. This street forms part of the Middletown area of Skipton, built between 1860 and 1910 when there was a rapid rise in the population of the town.

THE BOTTOM OF GREENSIDE with Eller Beck in the foreground. Note the pigeon loft.

CLUBHOUSES, a row of cottages so called because it was built by members of the Tradesmen's Sick Club. The Eller Beck flows at the front. Clubhouses was demolished in 1958.

NEWMARKET STREET COTTAGES that have since been demolished. The man with the barrow is Billy Gellin who scavaged in the canal for coal from the boats. Billy was known never to wear a shirt, but he attended church every Sunday in a top hat given to him by Mr Brumfitt, the undertaker.

SWADFORD STREET looking towards Belle Vue Mill. The Ship Hotel is on the right. On the corner on the left stood the original Christ Church vicarage.

SWADFORD HOUSE, in the centre, was built by Samuel John Swire in the early eighteenth century. It was acquired in 1928 by Skipton Co-operative Society who, at the time when this photograph was taken, already owned premises on either side of it. The door on the right, next to the poster, led to the Co-op office and boardroom.

SWADFORD STREET before 1888. A cast-iron urinal stands at the corner of the post office site and at the end of that row is the Old Ship Hotel, replaced by a larger building in 1888. The large house on the right was Grange's confectionery shop.

ENTRANCE TO THE CASTLE WOODS.

DAMAGE IN THE CASTLE WOODS, caused by the flood of 3 June 1908.

# The Town at Work

MR DIXON, manager of the grocery department of the Sackville Street Co-op.

SKIPTON TRADESMEN in charge of the ox-roasting held to mark the coronation of King Edward VII in 1902. Back row, left to right: James Whittaker, butcher; G. Aldersley; J. Phillip, butcher; Mr Foulds, Co-op manager; Inspector Randerson, weights and measures; Mr Boothman, butcher; Mr Helm, grocer. Front row, left to right: Mr Tasker; -?-; E. Smith, butcher.

SIMPSON'S TAILORS, on Swadford Street, the workroom.

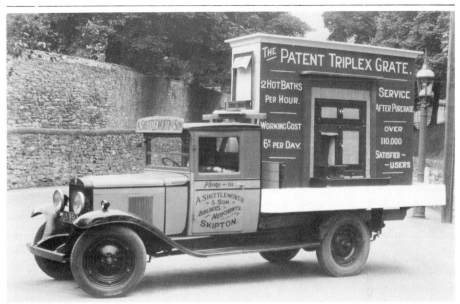

GALA FLOAT advertising A. Shuttleworth & Son, Builders Merchants. The firm was noted for fireplaces and for plastering.

MR WARD'S SMITHY on Raikes Road. In the centre is Mr Ward and on his left Mr Beck. The sign bears the name of A. Ellwood, Mr Ward's uncle, from whom he took over the business.

THOMAS SPENCER (1851–1905), born in Queen's Court, Skipton, co-founder of Marks & Spencer. Tom Spencer was the son of John Spencer, shoemaker, and his wife, the former Miss Elizabeth Horner. He left Skipton for Leeds in about 1870 and became bookkeeper for the firm of Isaac Dewhirst. It was Dewhirst who suggested that he went into partnership with Michael Marks who wanted to set up a limited company. Spencer contributed three hundred pounds for his half-share.

THE ENTRANCE TO CASTLE WOODS, known locally as Skipton Woods. On the right are the remains of the Castle Wood yard. High Mill was built in this area, the first textile mill in Skipton.

WORKERS AT THE SILK MILL on Sackville Street in January 1909. The mill, adapted in about 1896 for the manufacture of silk by C.A. Rickards Ltd, of Airton, had been seriously damaged by fire in November 1908 and was eventually demolished.

THE CASTLE ESTATE CREOSOTE TANK in Skipton Castle Woods. Local people with chest troubles were advised to stand near the tank and breathe deeply.

ROCK LINE WORKINGS at Skipton's Hawbank Quarry, from a sketch by Mrs E. Illingworth made in the 1930s. In the foreground is the line by which stone was taken to the loading bays on the Springs Canal.

SKIPTON ROCK QUARRY, where high-quality limestone has been quarried for over two hundred years. Writing of the quarry in 1852, Benson Bailey stated that it employed from sixty to eighty men and that the method of getting the stone was by means of 'falls' from which 25,000 to 30,000 tons at a time were dislodged by explosions.

SPRINGS CANAL LOADING CHUTES where limestone from Skipton Rock was transferred to canal boats. Extreme care was needed in loading, otherwise the boat could be extensively damaged.

SPRINGS CANAL, repairing damage after the flood of 3 June 1908. As the result of a storm on Rylstone Fell, the Eller Beck flooded and smashed through the Castle Woods, bursting two dams and flooding the towpath of the canal to a depth of 2 or 3 feet.

BOATS ON THE SPRINGS CANAL. The chutes for loading limestone can be seen in the background.

LONG DAM, Eller Beck and the Springs Canal in the Castle Woods. A boat is being towed along the canal by a local man known as Tommy 'Often'. Tradition states that he received sixpence (2½p) a trip.

HIGH CORN MILL and the Springs Canal from a sketch by Griff Hollingshead. There was a corn mill on this site from medieval times to the 1980s. This building is still in use as commercial premises.

CANAL BOAT on the Leeds–Liverpool Canal near Belmont Bridge.

CANAL BOAT on the Leeds–Liverpool Canal near Bank Newton. The canal towpaths in the vicinity of Skipton are very picturesque.

DREDGER DOING MAINTENANCE WORK on the Leeds–Liverpool Canal at the canal basin, the junction of the Leeds–Liverpool Canal and Springs Canal.

THIS BUILDING, in about 1842, was a worsted spinning mill occupied by Mr Hallam, who sold it in 1872 to the Dewhursts. In 1882 it was being used as a spindle works, making spindles for the local textile industry. It has since been demolished.

WALLER HILL COTTAGES, by Gallows footbridge, after they had been taken over by Thorntons, Slaters. The site is now part of the bus station car park.

JOHN BONNY DEWHURST (1819–1904), son of John Dewhurst, the founder of Belle Vue Mills. A director of Dewhurst & Sons, Ltd, John Bonny was at various times chairman of the directors of the English Sewing Cotton Company, a member of the first local board of health, chairman of the governors of Ermysted's grammar school, a governor of the girls' high school, a trustee of the Sylvester Petyt's charity and chairman of Skipton Urban District Council. He was involved in local government for forty-six years.

CAKE IN THE SHAPE OF BELLE VUE MILLS made for a directors' dinner in about 1926. The mill was built in 1828 as a woollen mill. It was burnt to the ground on 2 January 1831, but reopened within the year as a cotton mill. The fire was thought to be the work of an arsonist, but no one was charged with this offence. The mill was extended in 1852, 1863/4 and 1867/70.

ROTO CONING IN THE 'COP SHOP'.

UNION SQUARE ENTRANCE. The Square was built in the early nineteenth century by a building club. It was intended to provide housing for the town's growing manufacturing population. Handloom weaving was carried on in the upper storeys of these houses.

UNION SQUARE photographed not long before its transformation into a warehouse by being gutted and roofed over, leaving only the outer walls.

DALES BUS ON WATER STREET. The sides are decorated with photographs of the Dales beauty spots.

GALA FLOAT advertising A. Shuttleworth & Son, Builders Merchants of Coach Street, and later of Water Street.

THE CARR FAMILY. G.E. Carr, seated in the centre, established a grocery business in Newmarket Street in 1886. Eventually the firm had twenty-eight branches in ten centres and employed a staff of 200. They were known as 'divi shops', paying 3s. 6d. in the pound (17½p) every quarter.

CARRS BAKERY, abutting on to the Leeds–Liverpool Canal. Baking was added to the firm's activities and they supplied shops as far afield as Morecambe. They were the first firm in the district to supply wrapped bread.

ONE OF G.E. CARR LTD'S VANS.

G.E. CARR LTD LORRY delivering flour.

PART OF THE FLEET of thirty vehicles belonging to Carrs, Grocers.

BAXTER AND WROE'S GARAGE on Newmarket Street, the local agents for Rolls Royce. The premises became the telephone exchange in 1954.

H. LISTER'S NEWSAGENTS SHOP on Keighley Road, with the proprietor standing in the doorway. This was a very small but well-patronized shop which also repaired umbrellas. There is still a newsagents on the site.

HOLGATE'S NURSERY on Sackville Street. The little shop has sold sweets, groceries, green-grocery and gifts, and is now a hairdresser's salon.

THE SHOP IN COACH STREET of T. Farnell, described in 1907 as a 'general and artistic wood carver, modern, antique, gothic'.

CENTRAL PREMISES of Skipton Co-operative Society, Swadford Street. Skipton Co-op was established in 1861, the first secretary being G.H. Cragg. This set of premises was opened in the 1920s. The assembly room was above.

DUKE STREET, one of the eight branches the Co-op formerly had in Skipton.

THE SWADFORD STREET CO-OP celebrating its Golden Jubilee in 1911. The banner reads, 'This is our Jubilee Year. May they attain theirs', a reference to King George V and Queen Mary.

CO-OPERATIVE BAKERY VAN outside the Sackville Street branch. G. Milner stands at the horse's head.

DUKE STREET BRANCH OF THE CO-OP. Two Chinese figures in the window are advertising tea.

IN THE CO-OP HALL on the retirement of Matron Higgins from Granville Street hospital. At a sale of work and tea in her honour, she is seen inspecting a set of pans.

SKIPTON STATION on the Midland line. The station, built in 1878, replaced an earlier structure at Anna Hills, nearer the town centre. Note the beautiful ironwork, some of which is still in place.

STAFF OF LADY PORTERS on Skipton station during the First World War.

G. SUTHERLAND'S SHOP, 3 Sheep Street, displaying seasonable fare.

FREARSON'S IRONMONGERS, on New-market Street.

BOOTHMAN'S BUTCHERS on Sheep Street. Thomas Boothman stands on the right. For many years the business had its own slaughterhouse in a croft on Gargrave Road. The shop closed in 1965 on the retirement of William, Robert and Edna Boothman.

HENRY ALCOCK, the solicitor, died in 1869. He had an extensive professional connection in Skipton and Craven and his firm still continues as Charlesworth, Wood and Brown. He was the first chairman of the local board of health and a guardian of the workhouse. He owned a great deal of property and the former Chancery Lane in Skipton got its name because it belonged to him.

IAIN MACLEOD (1913–1970) was appointed Chancellor of the Exchequer in the Heath Government in 1970, but died the same year at 11 Downing Street. He was born at Clifford House, Skipton, son of Dr Macleod, and was a pupil at St Monica's convent kindergarten and Ermysted's grammar school.

W.H. DAWSON (1860–1948), editor of the *Craven Pioneer* newspaper and author of *The History of Skipton,* published in 1882. In 1905 Dawson took up a government appointment under Lloyd George and made a special study of social conditions in Germany, preparatory to the introduction of the National Health Insurance Scheme into this country.

LORD MORAN (1882–1977), born in Skipton in a house in High Street opposite the parish church. The second son of Dr John Forsythe Wilson, he was Sir Winston Churchill's personal physician for many years.

OPENING OF THE NEW CATTLE MARKET on 28 May 1906 in the Jerry Croft behind the town hall. The croft was formerly part of the farm lands belonging to the Red Lion public house in the High Street and it was also the site of a fun fair held two or three times a year.

LAYING ELECTRICITY CABLES at the bottom of Shortbank Road in about 1922. The current was switched on in Skipton on 12 September 1923.

OFFICERS OF THE 2/6 BATTALION, Duke of Wellington's Regiment, 1 September 1939.

LAYING THE STONE of the Ambulance Hall, Skipton, c. 1930.

# Religious and Cultural Life

CRAVEN NATURALIST AND SCIENTIFIC ASSOCIATION on its first field trip in summer, 1887. The association was founded in March 1887 and still flourishes.

PARISH CHURCH OF THE HOLY TRINITY, Skipton. The earliest mention of a church in the town is in the early twelfth century. The present building, which has been enlarged and altered over the years, is in the robust style generally known as 'Pennine perpendicular'. The gravestones have been removed from the front and placed along the wall at the rear of the building.

CHANCEL SCREEN DOOR of the parish church. The screen, reputed to have come from Bolton Priory, was erected in 1533.

TOMB OF GEORGE CLIFFORD, (1558–1605), third Earl of Cumberland and father of Lady Anne Clifford, who restored the castle and the church after the Civil War. The tomb is noteworthy in being ornamented by what is reputedly the most elaborate assemblage of noble bearings to be found on any tomb in England. The third Earl was a licensed buccaneer under Queen Elizabeth I, and took part in the fight against the Spanish Armada.

TOMB OF HENRY CLIFFORD (1493–1542), first Earl of Cumberland. Dawson in his *History of Skipton* wrote, 'It will be seen, therefore, that in Skipton church have been interred the bodies of five earls, three countesses and four earls' sons'.

PARISH CHURCH LECTERN, presented in memory of Thomas and Ann Mitchell of Skipton in 1881.

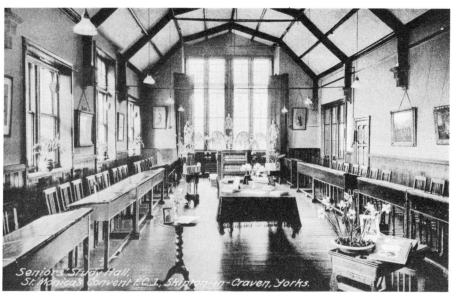

ST MONICA'S CONVENT SCHOOL, the senior study hall. The convent was established in 1861 and the school, a Roman Catholic boarding and day school, provided excellent tuition for boys aged five to eight years and for girls up to the age of eighteen.

WATER STREET WESLEYAN METHODIST CHURCH. Built in 1864 to seat 900 people, it closed in 1952. The building, architecturally one of the finest in the town, is now used as offices. Behind the chapel is the primary school which was formerly the Wesleyan day school.

BROUGHTON ROAD PRIMITIVE METHODIST CHURCH, known as 't'owd tin tab'. A Primitive Methodist mission began in the Broughton Road area in 1902, and in 1906 this iron and wood building was erected. In 1950 it was superseded by a stone building on a site opposite, and is now a community centre.

MOUNT HERMON UNITED METHODIST CHURCH, Castle Street. This church was opened in 1878. In the latter part of its existence, the building was a Salvation Army citadel. It has now been demolished.

TRINITY METHODIST CHURCH, Westmoreland Street, celebrating its Golden Jubilee. The Revd Malarkey is in the centre.

MEN OF TRINITY METHODIST CHURCH don chefs' hats and aprons to serve at the tea table at Men's Weekend, c. 1929. Back row, left to right: B. Griffin; J. Davies; A. Bailey; -?-; C. Miles; F. Cleaver; -?-. Second row: B. Baythorpe; H. Bailey; W. Davies Senior; S. Southwell; E. Cleaver. Third row: J. Mewies; -?-; Mr Morgan; J. Newman; T. Savage; W. Cleaver; D. Mayman.

TRINITY METHODIST CHURCH nativity play, 1936. Left-hand side, standing: Laura Hodgson; -?-; Adeline Horner. Centre panel: Alice Crook. Cradle: Ivy Miles. Front: Ephsy Smith. Right-hand panel, back: Vera Davies; Florence Tillottson. Front: Violet Emmott; Anne Atkinson.

TRINITY METHODIST CHURCH HARVEST FESTIVAL DISPLAY.

CHAPEL OF THE KNIGHTS HOSPITALLERS which became Ermysted's grammar school in 1548. The grammar school was founded in 1492 by Peter Toller and re-founded in 1548 by William Ermysted, a canon residentiary of St Paul's and Master of the Temple. This building is now an electricity substation.

ERMYSTED'S GRAMMAR SCHOOL, the premises on Gargrave Road to which the school moved in 1877

ERMYSTED'S GRAMMAR SCHOOL, the view before the building of Park Avenue.

BROUGHAM STREET SCHOOL on an outing to Chester in about 1934.

AIREVILLE, built by Henry Alcock in 1836, later the home of the Dewhurst family and, from 1952, the nucleus of Aireville school which was formally opened by the Right Hon. Iain Macleod in 1958. The grounds of Aireville are now a public park.

CRAVEN NATURALIST AND SCIENTIFIC ASSOCIATION at Coniston Hall in 1950, the home of Colonel Tottie, an enthusiastic member.

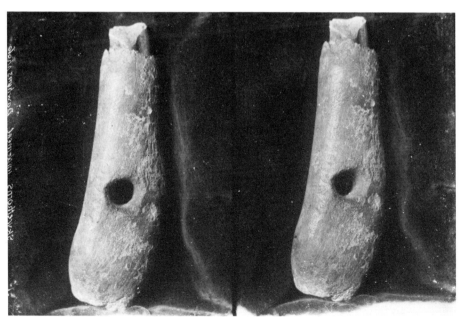

BONE CHISEL IN ANTLER SOCKET of about 6700BC found in August 1893 in Calf Hole cave, Skyrethorns by the Revd E. Jones. The original tool, the only one of its kind found in Britain, was in a briefcase stolen from a Manchester railway station. Fortunately, photographs had been taken and replicas made, one of which is in the Craven Museum.

MR BOWLES, who laid out the grounds of Ermysted's grammar school. Gargrave Road.

HANDING OVER THE CRAVEN MUSEUM to Skipton UDC on 4 April 1934. F.J. North Dufty makes the presentation to Councillor J. Daley. The museum, then housed in the public library, originally was the property of the Craven Museum and Archaelogical Society and was first opened to the public in 1928. It is now accommodated in a purpose-built annexe of the town hall.

SKIPTON MALE VOICE CHOIR.

SKIPTON MISSION BAND, founded by Jack Guy as part of his work in the Christian Mission, Skipton. The band had already enjoyed a long and successful life when it changed its name to Skipton Prize Band in 1919. It is still in existence today.

SKIPTON AMATEUR DRAMATIC SOCIETY, c. 1910.

THE FIRST OLD AGE PENSIONS COMMITTEE, 1909. Back row, left to right: J. Dodgson; J. Slingsby; Mr Driver; -?-; Mr Wilson; Mr Parkinson. Front row: J. Platt; Mr Fletcher; -?-; T.E. Edmondson; R.G. Rankin.

# SECTION FOUR

# Leisure

START OF A RECHABITE FRIENDLY SOCIETY TRIP on the Leeds–Liverpool canal from Skipton to Farnhill in the early 1920s. The boats usually carried coal, flour or sugar and had to be cleaned for the occasion. Chapmans builders yard is in the background, at the junction of Sackville Street with Keighley Road.

THE SHIP HOTEL in Swadford Street before rebuilding in 1888. On the right was the china and glassware shop of Baldisarro Porri.

THE NAG'S HEAD in Newmarket Street which lost its licence in 1909 and became the Nag's Head Fisheries. It was demolished in 1966.

WARSHIP WEEK during the Second World War. Mr Yeoman walks alongside the 'battleship' outside the town hall.

VJ CELEBRATION PARTY in Back Devonshire Street, August 1945.

DOYLE'S BRIDGE on the edge of the Castle Woods, a favourite place for a stroll. This view is now crossed by a bypass.

THE BOAT *ALEXANDRA II* with trippers on board. In the background is a canal warehouse which is now converted to a shop but retains some of its original features.

THE 'SWEETPEA CLUB'. Each of the young men wears a sweetpea in his buttonhole, but the club appears to have been based on residence in the Park Hill and Gargrave Road area, rather than an interest in horticulture.

CO-OPERATIVE SOCIETY FIELD DAY, 1906.

CHARABANC OUTING in the 1920s; a party of Skiptonians in a 'toast rack' vehicle at Blackpool.

FRANK MARSDEN, founder of Marsden & Naylor's iron foundry, preparing to set off in his car from 12 Firth Street.

NIFFANY ROVERS ASSOCIATION FOOTBALL CLUB. The team took its name from Niffany Farm, Broughton Road and played on Niffany Fields.

SKIPTON CRICKET CLUB, 1908, at Sandylands playing fields. Back row, left to right: Jack Smith; O. Hall; N. Robinson; D. Robinson. Second row: -?-; Foster Horner; Billy Greenwood (Captain); H. Geldard; F. Furness. Front row: A. Girling; H. Watson.

MOOR VIEW BATHS before the introduction of mixed bathing. There are changing cubicles on one side only. Later a door was made in the end wall for bathers to go to the outdoor pool.

SKIPTON AMATEUR SWIMMING CLUB at Moor View Baths in 1911. Mr Geoffreys, baths manager and instructor, stands on the right.

ANNUAL SWIMMING GALA at the outdoor pool in 1900. The pool was a converted reservoir.

GALA DAY DOG SHOW in the 1940s. On the left is G. Rickards MP; fourth from the left is George Leatt of Skipton, an internationally famous judge of dogs.

GALA DAY in 1911. The gala started in 1901 to raise funds for Skipton hospital on Granville Street, erected to mark the Diamond Jubilee of 1897.

GALA FLOAT from Trinity Wesleyan church, depicting Grace Darling's fishing boat, complete with lighthouse and cottonwool snow.

THE FLOAT which won second prize in the gala of 1916. Note the elaborately decorated horse.

SKIPTON UDC GAS DEPARTMENT joined in with a float showing a gas cooker. The slogan on the front reads, 'No Smell, No Dirt, No Trouble', and that on the side, 'Make Light of Your Labour. Our Labour Makes Light'. The council bought Skipton Gas Company in 1899.

GALA PROCESSION on Mill Bridge in the 1950s.

GALA QUEEN and retinue in 1949. Left to right: Dorothy Bateman; Margaret O'Brien; Mavis Feather; -?-; -?-; Shirley Beard.

BULLOCKS AND WAGON being brought round Duckett Street with East Castle Street on to Westmoreland Street to join the gala procession.

GALA PROCESSION passing Highfield Terrace, c. 1912. The railway sidings can just be seen on the right.

TRINITY WESLEYAN METHODIST CHURCH gala float in 1914. Horner's grocers shop is in the background on the right.

# Villages I

CROSS HILLS, Main Street, decorated for the coronation of King George V in 1911. The gas showroom (Kildwick Parish Gas Company) is on the right and the Yorkshire Penny Bank on the left.

SUTTON HALL in Sutton-in-Craven. The Hall was built in about 1894 and was for a time the home of J.W. Hartley, owner of Greenroyd Mill. It was demolished in the late 1930s.

SUTTON-IN-CRAVEN PARK, opened in 1912 on land given by two mill owners, J.W. Hartley and James Bairstow. The Baptist church is in the background. The kidney-shaped paddling pool is in the foreground.

SUTTON-IN-CRAVEN BAPTIST CHURCH, rebuilt and reopened in 1865. This building was demolished in about 1968 to make way for a new building on the same site.

MR THOMAS of Sutton-in-Craven who chopped logs to be sold for Baptist church funds.

WAINMANS BOTTOM, Cowling Beck, showing the footbridge below Carr Head.

RIDGE MILL BRIDGE over Cowling Beck, destroyed some years ago in a flood.

LUMB MILL BRIDGE and mill buildings at Glusburn.

CROSS HILLS, Main Street. The gabled building on the right was St John's Sunday school, then an organ-maker's workshop. It is now a supermarket. There is a blacksmith's shop on the left with a sign advertising 'Carburine Motor Spirit'.

CROSS HILLS, Main Street, with B.H. Wilson, ironmonger and tinsmith on the left. The tall building on the left was the premises of the co-op. The sign of the umbrella and spectacles on the right marked Emott's opticians, clock repairers and jewellers. Thornton's grocers is the first shop on the right.

CROSS HILLS, Main Street, showing setts at the top of Holme Lane.

ROGER NICHOLSON'S WHEELWRIGHTS SHOP in Cross Hills, Main Street, c. 1900. The site is now an amenity area. Left to right: -?-, -?-, Roger Nicholson (proprietor), -?-, Sylvester Green, Fred Hargreaves, Harry Riley (apprentice wheelwright), John Nicholson (proprietor's son).

CROSS HILLS, Main Street, in 1911. On the left is an electric pole for the trackless tram.

FLOAT, 'THE BRITISH EMPIRE', on the showfield at Holme Lane, 1911. Atkinson's corn mill chimney is in the background.

CROSS HILLS, Holme Lane, before 1909 when the road was widened and the grass verge on the left disappeared. The chimney is probably that of H. & T. Riddiough's steam-driven saw mill and joinery on Lothersdale Road.

CROSS HILLS, Holme Lane. On the right can be seen poles that formed part of the Cedes-Stoll trackless car system which operated in the village from 1915 to 23 May 1924.

CROSS HILLS, Lothersdale Road, with Ablemarle Cottage on the right and a shop (possibly Stow's) on the left.

CROSS HILLS, Station Lane, in 1911. The lane led to Kildwick and Cross Hills railway station. Bank House, the old post office, is on the left. On the right are the premises of Greenwoods, plasterers and contractors, who carried out some of the decorative work at the Alhambra Theatre, Bradford.

DANCING IN CROSS HILLS, Main Street, to celebrate the coronation of 1911. On the extreme left is Holly Bank, later a doctor's surgery. On the right is Parker's, formerly Lund's, saddlers and harnessmakers, and to the left of that is J. Roberts, bakers.

CROSS HILLS, Keighley Road. Spencer's shop on the right is now the post office, the third in the village. The trees in the background have disappeared.

JOHN GREENWOOD, of Cross Hills won all these trophies on 19 July 1913 for swimming and diving in the Kildwick Aire Bridge swimming carnival. The gold watch at the front of the table is still in the possession of his family.

THE WINDOW OF GREEN & PETTY, tailors, in Cross Hills, Main Street, decorated for the coronation of 1911. Note the two photographers in the foreground.

GLUSBURN, decorative arch across Colne Road between Hayfield Mill on the left and the Institute grounds on the right.

GLUSBURN OLD HALL, thought to date from the early seventeenth century. The tower is a nineteenth-century addition.

GLUSBURN INSTITUTE, opened on 8 October 1892, built as an 'Educational, Social, and Religious centre for the life of the village' by Sir John C. Horsfall.

REV. GEORGE ARMITT

GLUSBURN INSTITUTE AND . . . MISSION HALL . . .

THE INSTITUTE.

GLUSBURN INSTITUTE, showing the addition of a mission hall for the Baptist church.

GLUSBURN INSTITUTE in 1908 during the building of the baths and clock tower.

LOTHERSDALE, the Quaker meeting house, built c. 1776 to replace a smaller building of 1721. In 1795 eight Lothersdale Quakers were arrested for non-payment of tithes and church dues. Their captivity in York Castle lasted for two years and five months, and one of them died in prison. Another died soon after his release when the parish constable took his bed from under him in order to sell it. Lothersdale Meeting ceased in 1958.

LOTHERSDALE, Brigstone, the home of Joseph Brown (1751–1803), Quaker, drystone waller and poet. Joseph was one of the friends imprisoned at York in 1795.

LOTHERSDALE, the barytes mine, from a photograph of 1892 by Sir Benjamin Stone.

LOTHERSDALE, Wilson's cotton mill at Dale End showing the 45 ft diameter water wheel, installed in 1850. The wheel can still be viewed by interested parties.

ANIMAL REMAINS FROM THE RAYGILL FISSURE. Remains are shown of *Elephas antiquus, Rhinoceros leptor Linus, Cervus capreolus, Felis leo* var. *spelaea,* bear, bison, hyena, hippopotamus and roebuck. This particular collection was destroyed when the quarry office burnt down. Photograph c. 1930.

LOTHERSDALE, Raygill fissure in 1930. The fissure, which is on the south side of Raygill Quarry, was explored by the Yorkshire Geological Society in the 1880s. It has since been quarried away.

LOTHERSDALE, Raygill House. This was the home of the Spencer family, with whom Sir Benjamin Stone was friendly and who he visited on many occasions. The Spencers experimented with and patented many improvements to limekilns, using Raygill as a base. In the foreground are 'landscaped' quarry and mine tips.

LOTHERSDALE, Raygill limekilns. From left to right, Rover kiln, number one kiln and number two kiln. The Rover kiln was at one time experimentally gas fired.

CONONLEY LEAD MINE, the engine house and chimney erected in the 1830s.

LIMEKILN on the roadside near Cononley Lane End between the canal and the road. The site was reused by the Sibsey family, blacksmiths of Gargrave, who set up a temporary forge there on market days.

CONONLEY, mine offices in Nethergill.

CONONLEY RAILWAY STATION, recently reopened.

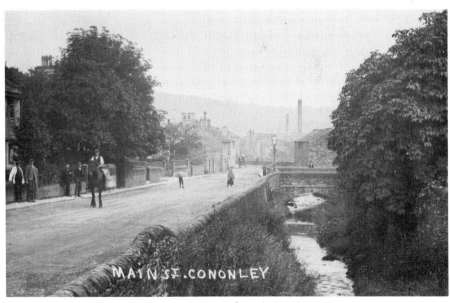

THE MAIN STREET of Cononley looking towards Green's Aireside Mill.

OLD AGE PENSIONERS AT FARNHILL, c. 1908.

FARNHILL, looking down the main street.

FARNHILL MILL, after the fire of 20 December 1905.

KILDWICK, Airedale Mill, after the fire of 31 March 1906.

KILDWICK, Airedale Mill, on the south side of the road between Kildwick and Cononley Lane End.

THE INTERIOR OF AIREDALE MILL, Kildwick, after the fire. All trace of this mill has now disappeared.

KILDWICK from Station Road in Cross Hills. Houses have now been built in the field on the left.

THE PARISH CHURCH OF ST ANDREW, Kildwick, and the White Lion public house in 1911.

THE PARISH CHURCH OF ST ANDREW during restoration work in 1902. The Kildwick church is known as 'the Lang Kirk of Craven' and at $145\frac{1}{2}$ ft is is one of the longest churches in Yorkshire.

KILDWICK from the River Aire with the medieval bridge and the large pool on the right where the swimming gala and yearly carnival was held in July. The new building in the centre is now a church hostel, rededicated in 1930.

KILDWICK HALL GATEWAY with the old court house on the left. Legend has it that the stone lions go down to the river to drink at midnight.

# Villages II

EMPLOYEES OF SLINGSBYS COTTON MILL, Carleton, c. 1900. Back row, first left: John Lawson. Second row, second left: George Brown.

CARLETON IN THE AIRE VALLEY. The chimneys are those of Slingsby Mills.

SHEEP WASHING AT SMITHY BRIDGE, Carleton in 1907.

CARLETON SCHOOL CHILDREN. Back row, left to right: Miss Edith Lilley; -?-; Sam Shaw; Ernest Shaw; Henry Preston; Norman Preston; Maurice Preston; Wilfred Dale; Miss Rose Lilley. Second row: Edith Bradley; William Naylor; Daisy Shaw; Edward Higgins; -?-; Martha Hartley; Minnie (Lynn) Hutchinson; Alan Smith; Jessie Orcherton. Third row: Kitty Kay; John Overend; Minnie Ware; Wilfred Hey; Dorothy Ayrton; William Shaw; Vina Wane. Front row: Tommy Higgins; Lizzie Higgins; Nellie Jackson; -?-; Nellie Orcherton.

CARLETON GIRL'S FRIENDLY SOCIETY, c. 1914.

CARLETON CO-OPERATIVE SOCIETY FIELD DAY, 24 June 1907.

CARLETON FEAST, swingboats and stalls near the Swan Inn. Carleton Mill is in the background.

THE PREMISES OF J.J. SMITH, fruit dealer, later became Carleton post office.

SUNNY BANK, Carleton, built on the site of the less romantically named Dog Row.

CARLETON ASSOCIATION FOOTBALL CLUB, 1907/8.

CARLETON UNITED ASSOCIATION FOOTBALL CLUB, 1909/10.

CARLETON SILVER JUBILEE CELEBRATIONS, 1935.

ST MARY'S CHURCH, Carleton, choir and confirmation candidates in the late 1930s.

HAMBLETHORPE FARM, Bradley, with Mr Throup ploughing.

BRADLEY, plough team resting. Joe Throup and his son Frank sit under the wall.

HAYMAKING in Bradley around the turn of the century.

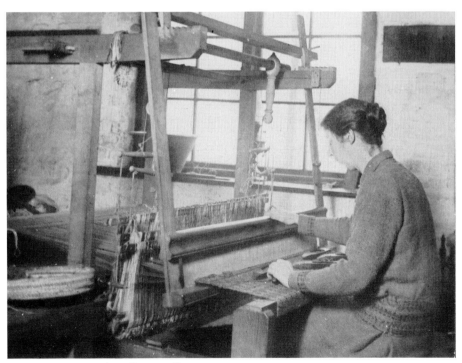

HAND-LOOM WEAVING in a Craven village.

WHIT WALK IN PROGRESS AT WEST VIEW, Bradley. Wesleyan and Primitive Methodists held walks in the village at Whitsuntide.

BRADLEY COUNCIL SCHOOL with Mr Edwin Bray, headmaster between 1896 and 1923, with a class of boys. This photograph was probably taken in 1914, not long after the new school building was opened.

BRADLEY CRICKET CLUB, winners of the Skipton Junior League cup in 1907.

CRAVEN HUNT outside the Bay Horse, Bradley.

THE SWEET WILLIAM LODGE of the Independent Order of the Golden Fleece outside the Slater's Arms, Bradley. The Lodge was founded in 1862.

LOOKING TOWARDS LIDGET BOTTOM, Bradley and the Primitive Methodist chapel, built in 1897. The man with his dog is probably farmer, John Walker.

WEDDING OF JOSEPH BREAR AND ETHEL HOLGATE at Bradley.

BRADLEY MAIN STREET, with Smith Green's greengrocery cart.

CRAG LANE, Bradley.

BRADLEY POST OFFICE, with a Silver Star bus parked opposite.

THE REVD EDMUND JONES, Swedenborgian Minister of Embsay and a keen antiquary, in Elbolton Cave in 1888. Mr Jones, known as 'Bishop Bones', is standing at the foot of the ladder in the excavation area which yielded important Neolthic and Bronze Age remains. This excavation was undertaken by the Craven Naturalists, the society he was instrumental in founding.

EMBSAY MANOR, a picturesque seventeenth-century building, for a time the home of Halliwell Sutcliffe, the Dales novelist.

EMBSAY, showing the station on the Skipton to Ilkley line.

GOOD INTENT FARM, Embsay, demolished to make way for the reservoir. The water treatment plant was built on the site. Mr and Mrs Wellock can be seen at the garden gate. Grouse Cottage is in the background on the right.

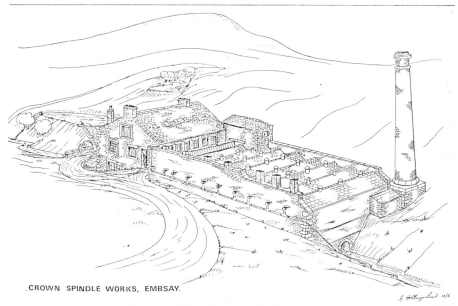

CROWN SPINDLE WORKS, EMBSAY.

CROWN SPINDLE WORKS, Embsay. The oldest part of these premises date from 1826. Bayonets were made here during the Crimean War.

CROWN SPINDLE WORKS, Embsay, now private houses.

WHITFIELD, Embsay, a hamlet drowned when Embsay reservoir was built in 1910.

SCENE DURING THE CONSTRUCTION OF EMBSAY RESERVOIR in 1910. Miss M. Phillip of the Old Post Office, Embsay, photographed every stage in the building of the reservoir.

BUILDING OF EMBSAY RESERVOIR, mixing cement. Note the tarpaulin screens to keep off the worst of the bad weather.

BUILDING OF EMBSAY RESERVOIR, banking hands dressing stone and building slipway.

57
J. FOWLER STEAM ENGINE used in the construction of Embsay reservoir, drawing a trailer on which is a saddle tank engine.

HALLIWELL SUTCLIFFE (1870–1932), at the wheel of his car in Embsay, where he lived for a time after his marriage. Sutcliffe published numerous novels based on the Dales and was also an expert on the local dialect.

DRAUGHTON VILLAGE, between Skipton and Addingham, in quieter times. The village is now bypassed.

THE MATCHLESS INN, Draughton. The inn was built with the winnings from the racehorse, Matchless, in the early nineteenth century. Standing in front of the inn are, from left to right: Mrs Riley; the servant; Mrs Riley's son Joe.

EASTBY, the sanatorium, dating from the early years of this century, but closed during the Second World War.

BOLTON ABBEY, the Devonshire Arms Hotel.

KING GEORGE V AND QUEEN MARY arriving at Bolton Abbey station to stay with the Duke of Devonshire for the shooting.

GARGRAVE, Airebank Mill, formerly a cotton mill, Johnson & Johnson's since 1934.

GARGRAVE, the bridge over the River Aire, looking towards St Andrew's church.

GARGRAVE, the fountain.

G.D. HUNT of Gargrave in his shoemaker's shop. Mr Hunt's father, James, moved to Gargrave in 1860 and was apprenticed to Abraham Bateson, shoemaker.

GARGRAVE, before the removal of the war memorial to its present site.

GARGRAVE.

ST ANDREW'S CHURCH, Gargrave, from a painting of about 1828.

A QUIET CORNER OF GARGRAVE, near the church.

NEW BRIGHTON SAW MILL, near Gargrave, the 'making' department. Tennis rackets were made at New Brighton. The same premises were later used by Rice Caravans.

POLISHING SHOP, New Brighton saw mill.

STRINGING SHOP, New Brighton saw mill.

FINISHING SHOP, New Brighton saw mill.

WEST MARTON, the double-arched bridge over the Leeds–Liverpool Canal, with *Alexandra II*.

ELSLACK MOOR, the beacon watcher's stone. The inscription reads, 'Here was found dead the body of Robert Wilson, one of the Beacon Guards, who died January 29 1805, aged 59 years'. During the dark days of a threatened French invasion Robert Wilson was frozen to death when returning from Elslack to the beacon watcher's hut on Pinhaw with provisions. He was less than 150 yards from safety.

THE *ARTHUR OF SKIPTON* on the Leeds–Liverpool Canal in Craven.

THE LEEDS–LIVERPOOL CANAL at West Marton.

LIGHT WEIGHT CYCLE CAR of the 1920s on the road to Rylstone. The car was built by Graham White & Co. Ltd.

TOLL HOUSE of 1853 at Sandybeck Bar, the road from Skipton to Rylstone.

RUINED BARN AT BARDEN near the junction of the Bolton Abbey and Embsay roads. This ling-thatched cruck barn was dismantled and re-erected at Shibden Hall Museum, Halifax, but was burnt down soon after.

PAST AND PRESENT MEMBERS of the Friends of the Craven Museum excavating an eighteenth-century tilery at Rylstone in the early 1970s. Left to right: John Gunby; Rosemary Payne; C.A. Smith; Thelma Hall; Dr Arthur Raistrick; -?-; Cathy Harrison; Georgina Crossland; Percy Baldwin; Helen Ward.

# ACKNOWLEDGEMENTS

It would have been impossible to compile this book without a great deal of help from many people. The Friends of the Craven Museum are particularly grateful to those who suppied us with information for the captions and to the following members, friends and institutions who kindly lent photographs or gave us permission to use photographs of which they hold the copyright. If we have overlooked anyone in the latter category, please accept our apologies for the omission:

Mrs E. Bannister ● Mr W. Bean ● Miss Daphne Brown ● Mr Allan Butterfield
Mr R. Carr ● *Craven Herald* newspaper ● Craven Museum ● Craven Naturalist
and Scientific Association ● Mr and Mrs J. Gunby ● Mr and Mrs A. Harrison
Mr J. Holden ● Mr G. Hollingshead ● Mrs P. J. Mansergh ● Marks & Spencer plc
Mr P. Mawson ● Mr J. Middleton ● Mrs Margaret Moorehouse ● Miss R. O'Rourke
Mr Patchett ● Miss Doris Riley ● Mrs R.G. Rowley ● Mr C. A. Smith ● Mrs D. Tierney
Mrs E. Tyrer ● Mr and Mrs W.E. Walker ● Mr M. Walmsley ● Mr F. D. Woodall
Mr and Mrs W. Wright

Valentine Rowley and Peggy Walker deserve special thanks for having coped with the typing.